Books by John J. Loeper

GOING TO SCHOOL IN 1776

THE FLYING MACHINE
A Stagecoach Journey in 1774

THE SHOP ON HIGH STREET
The Toys and Games of Early America

THE GOLDEN DRAGON
By Clipper Ship Around the Horn

MR. MARLEY'S MAIN STREET CONFECTIONERY
A History of Sweets and Treats

GALLOPING GERTRUDE
By Motorcar in 1908

BY HOOK AND LADDER
The Story of Fire Fighting in America

BY HOOK & LADDER

The Story of
Fire Fighting in America

By Hook &

The Story of Fire
Fighting in America

Ladder

ILLUSTRATED
WITH
OLD PRINTS

by John J. Loeper

ATHENEUM   New York 1981

LIBRARY OF CONGRESS CATALOGING IN PUBLICATION DATA

Loeper, John J.
By hook and ladder.

SUMMARY: A brief history of American fire fighting
including information on firemen, female firefighters,
fire engines, fire fighting techniques and some
famous fires in American history.
  1. Fire extinction—Juvenile literature.
2. Fire fighters—Juvenile literature.   [1. Fire
extinction.   2. Fire fighters]   I. Title.
TH9148.L6   628.9′25   80-36738
ISBN 0-689-30816-7

To the brave men and women
of volunteer fire units

Contents

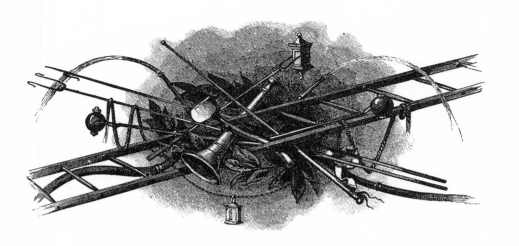

INTRODUCTION

The hook and ladder are symbols of fire fighting.

Since earliest times fire fighters have used hooks to "hook open" windows and to rip open walls. This allows the heat and smoke to escape. It also gives fire fighters access to the source of the fire.

If hooks save buildings, ladders save people. Ladders of every size help people out of burning buildings.

The hook and the ladder are among the oldest weapons used in fighting fire.

People have always feared fire. Uncontrolled, it can destroy life and property. Records are filled with accounts of disastrous fires. One of the earliest great fires burned down ancient Troy. In the second century B.C., the city of Carthage was completely destroyed by fire, and in the first century A.D. fire reduced most of ancient Rome to ruin. Throughout history most cities have experienced major fires. In 1666, "a horrid, bloody flame" destroyed over fourteen hundred buildings in London.

What has been called the first fire department in the world was organized in Rome in the first century A.D. The Roman *Vigiles* were a corps of night watchmen equipped with fire fighting apparatus. Centuries later, Marco Polo reported seeing fire fighting groups in Chinese cities. Throughout history, fighting destruction by fire has been one of mankind's great concerns.

In America the first fire departments were mostly volunteer "bucket brigades." Then came fire departments organized on a volunteer basis. Later on, many communities established paid fire departments.

The story of fires and fire fighting is both glamorous and deadly. To be a fire fighter calls for courage and dedication. It can be tough, dangerous work. More fire fighters are killed in the performance of duty than those involved in any other occupation. Yet, there is adventure. The sound of sirens, the leap of flames and the confrontation with danger makes it exciting.

More than three hundred fires occur every hour in the United States. And more than a million fire fighters make it their business to control these fires. These men and women continue a tradition of service that goes back to our country's beginning.

ONE OF OUR FIREMEN.

Behold the noble Fireman,
All dressed in red and black,
He climbs the tilted ladder
With a rope upon his back.
An axe he carries by his side,
A helmet on his head,
He goes to fight the fire,
Most powerful and dread.
He is our unsung hero,
This man of brawn and might,
And to watch him fight a fire
Is a great and wondrous sight.

FIREMAN'S SONG

1845

BY HOOK & LADDER

*The Story of
Fire Fighting in America*

Peter Stuyvesant's "Rattle Watch"

A wooden rattle was probably the first fire alarm in the new world. Peter Stuyvesant, the one-legged governor of the Dutch colony of New Amsterdam, established a "rattle watch." Volunteers patrolled the streets of the colony from darkness to dawn. At the first sign of a fire, they sounded the alarm with large wooden rattles.

The cry FIRE! brought terror to the hearts of the early settlers. With no fire fighting equipment, flames spread quickly, destroying flimsy houses of "board and bark." Jamestown, the first settlement in America, burned to the ground in 1608. Captain John Smith wrote in his journal: "our apparel, lodging and private possessions are all destroyed."

Fire fighting in America began with the Puritans in Boston. At the time, chimneys were made of wood lined with mud. Most houses had thatched roofs. As the mud chipped away with use, it exposed the wooden chimney to flames. And flying sparks often landed on the roofs. Thatch, being straw and dried grass, caught fire easily. Destruction of buildings was commonplace. About

1632, Boston officials ordered that "no Man shall build his chimney of wood, nor cover his house with thatch." This was America's first attempt to prevent fires.

But it was Peter Stuyvesant who organized fire fighting and fire prevention. In 1648, he passed a similar law —wooden chimneys and thatched roofs were forbidden— but enforced it by appointing fire wardens. These men, nicknamed "the prowlers," inspected buildings and levied fines against offenders. He ordered ladders and buckets to be kept "in readiness at the street corners" and asked citizens to keep buckets of water on their doorsteps "for the time of need."

The "prowlers" and "rattle watch" of New Amsterdam are among the forerunners of today's modern fire departments. From the beginning, fire fighting has been an important part of America's story.

Issac Joins the Bucket Brigade

In the early morning of October 10, 1720, Jacob Moore, baker of the New England village of Somerset, stoked his ovens. Chunks of oak and hickory wood provided fuel for the day's baking. His breads and rolls were eagerly awaited by the villagers. What was breakfast without a loaf of Mr. Moore's hot bread or a pan of his golden crusted rolls!

Using leather bellows, he stoked the flames. Proper baking needed a high temperature. As he pumped, a spark escaped and landed on a mound of straw. It was Missy's bed. Missy was the cat who kept the bakery free of marauding mice. Within seconds the straw bed ignited. Mr. Moore tried stamping the flames with his foot, but only succeeded in scattering the burning straw. A linen cloth caught fire, and smoke filled the room. The baker ran across the village green to the church. He pushed open the door and grabbed the bell rope. As he tugged, the bell pealed its warning to the village. In the small towns of early America, the church bell served many purposes. One of these was to sound the alarm in case of fire. The heads of sleepy villagers appeared at windows. Meanwhile the entire bakeshop seemed to be afire, and smoke filled the air.

"It's the bakery!" a man shouted.

"Grab your buckets!" another voice ordered.

Men, women and children rushed to the scene, some still wearing nightclothes.

"Take this bucket, Issac!" his mother demanded "and join the brigade!" Ten-year-old Issac, rubbing sleep from his eyes, took the bucket and ran toward the bakery.

The bucket brigade was one of the only ways people had to fight a fire. Two lines formed. One line of people passed filled buckets from a well or stream to the fire. Another line passed back the empty buckets to be re-filled. This constant supply of water, passed hand to hand, was thrown onto the flames. And everyone, young and old, was expected to help. Anyone who refused was an outcast. It was also an unwritten rule that no one crossed or broke the line of a bucket brigade. Fighting a fire was serious business.

"Keep 'em coming! Faster! Faster!" a man shouted.

Issac's arms ached as he swung the heavy buckets, one after another. Water splashed out onto his bare feet. The woman next to him scolded. "Don't waste the water!"

Before long, a voice cried out, "We've done it!"

The buckets stopped, and people cheered. The efforts of their bucket brigade had saved the bakery. The damage was not too great. The men of the village promised Mr. Moore that they would help with repairs. Mr. Moore would be back in business within the week.

"We'll be having burned toast for breakfast this morning," one woman joked.

With that, the face of Missy peered from behind a bush. She had returned from her morning walk, unaware of what had happened.

Issac went over and picked her up. "You can sleep in our barn until the bakery is repaired," he told her. She purred contentedly.

Then the call went out, "Claim your buckets!"

Issac found his bucket and returned home, wet and tired. Yet he was pleased that his work had been rewarded. The village was safe once again.

Benjamin Franklin's Bright Idea

"An ounce of prevention is worth a pound of cure!" Benjamin Franklin remarked to his friend. The two men sat at a table in the City Tavern in Philadelphia, discussing the recent fire at Bradbury's Wharf. It had destroyed several homes and warehouses.

"In Boston, groups of citizens have formed Fire Societies. The members promise to come to each other's aid in case of a fire," Franklin explained.

"It's an excellent idea," his friend answered. "We should try it here in Philadelphia. Why don't you organize it, Ben?"

"I have given it serious thought," Franklin said.

"And we need more than one fire engine, too," his friend added.

"I've suggested that in the *Gazette*," Franklin said. "And I will continue to press for better fire protection."

In the newspaper, *The Pennsylvania Gazette*, Franklin wrote:

"The wharf fire might have been prevented from spreading if the People had been provided with additional engines. The city is in danger while owning only one engine."

Franklin's words were heeded. Philadelphia ordered three additional fire engines. They arrived from London aboard the *Beaver* on December 3, 1731.

The fire engine is based on an old idea. In 200 B.C. a Greek named Ctesibius discovered that air under pressure can propel water and devised a pump. In the seventeenth century Ctesibius' idea was applied to fire fighting in Germany. A pumping machine was built that could shoot forth a stream of water with great force. The earliest fire engine of this type was in use in Nuremberg, Germany about 1657. The engine was drawn by two horses, and twenty-eight men were required to work the pumps.

In the eighteenth century, an Englishman, Richard Newsham, built a lighter and simplified version of the Nuremberg machine. This new machine, a pump and a water tank, was mounted on wheels and could be pulled to a fire. Buckets of water were dumped into the tank by one group of men while another group worked the pump. A stream of water shot out toward the fire. The earliest Newsham engines were pulled to a fire by hand. Later on, adaptations of the Newsham engine were built in America.

Although Boston boasted the first fire engine in

"OLD BLACK JOKE"
THE OLDEST HAND ENGINE IN THE U.S.

America, Philadelphia and New York owned pumpers as early as 1711.

In 1736 after much thought and planning, Benjamin Franklin organized a fire-fighting society. He and four friends formed the Union Fire Company. Each member promised to buy six leather buckets marked with the name of the company. The company provided other equipment at its own expense—engines, ladders, salvage bags and so on. When fire struck, the Union members rushed to the site. Some fought the blaze while others salvaged as many of the victims' possessions as possible. Unlike the Boston groups, the Union Fire Company served everybody, member or not. It was America's first volunteer fire company. Franklin was its first fire chief.

Franklin's idea caught on. Soon twelve other fire companies formed in Philadelphia, including the illustrious Hibernia Company. Made up largely of men of

Irish birth or heritage, its members included several signers of the Declaration of Independence.

In his *Autobiography*, Franklin wrote:

"I question whether there is a city in the world better provided with the means of fighting fires."

Another of Benjamin Franklin's ideas was the establishment of fire insurance. In 1752, he founded the Philadelphia Contributionship, the first successful fire insurance company in America.

Forms of fire insurance had existed in Europe, but it was largely an agreement among merchants to help each other in case of fire. Franklin's fire insurance was available to everyone. The company issued small metal disks to be attached to the outside wall of an insured building. These Fire Marks, as they were called, served notice that

FIREMARKS

the building was protected by insurance. As time passed, Franklin's idea spread. Fire insurance companies were formed in other parts of the country, and the companies took an active role in fire prevention.

Over two hundred years later, Philadelphia honored its first fire chief for his efforts in protecting the life and property of its citizens. The city placed a large bust of Franklin outside the fire station closest to Independence Hall. Created by sculptor Reginald Beauchamp, the bust is covered with 80,000 pennies donated by Philadelphia children. The pennies symbolize Franklin's adage, "A penny saved is a penny earned."

Boston in Flames

As a little boy, Benjamin Franklin witnessed the Boston fire of 1711. This fire burned for seven hours and left 110 families homeless. The disaster made a lasting impression on Franklin. But the city's worst fire occurred in 1760, while Franklin was living and working in Philadelphia.

On Thursday morning, March 20th, eleven-year-old Jeremiah Barr and his younger brother jumped out of bed. They were awakened by the noise of shouting in the street outside. Their bedroom smelled of smoke. Running to the window, they saw flames shooting from the roof of the house across the way. Then their bedroom door opened and their mother appeared. "Hurry, boys!" she ordered. "There is not much time." She grabbed some of their clothing and shoved it into a cloth bag.

They followed her downstairs where they met their father struggling with an armful of pots and pans.

"We must leave at once," he told them. "The house next door is already on fire."

They went out into the street. The air was heavy with smoke. People rushed about shouting and crying. One old woman wailed, "Boston is in flames!"

In 1760, the colonial city of Boston was a jumble of buildings housing nearly sixteen hundred people. Tucked among the houses were shops, warehouses and factories. Most of the structures were wooden with shingled roofs. There was hardly a building in the city that was not a

tinderbox. And when fire struck, the flames jumped across narrow streets from one building to another.

The fire started about two o'clock in the morning. Somebody saw the flames coming from the house of a Mrs. Jackson on Cornhill Street, and cries of FIRE awakened the neighbors, who rushed to the scene. Bucket brigades were formed, but the blaze was too fierce. The houses next to Mrs. Jackson's caught fire. In turn, they set fire to the houses next to them. Within minutes, five houses were burning. Soon, Boston's firefighters arrived, and the city's pumper was put into operation. But this effort began too late. The fire was out of control. Then a heavy wind came out of the northwest and spread the flames into the next block. Minutes later, the fire swept into other streets, lanes and alleys.

"In a seeming instant, all was flame," one eyewitness recorded. "Fire fell all around us."

The roaring wind picked up burning embers and hurled them around the city. Houses, shops and warehouses erupted in flames. The narrow streets of the city were jammed with people carrying their belongings. The town clerk reported that "the distressed inhabitants scarce knew where to take refuge from the devouring flames."

From a field on the outskirts of the city, Jeremiah and his family watched as the city burned. The fire raged for more than ten hours. A red glow could be seen for miles around. "Is our house gone?" Jeremiah asked his father.

"I'm sure it is, son," he answered sadly. "Along with most houses in the city."

His brother began to cry.

By late Thursday afternoon the fire had run its course. But large parts of the city were reduced to smoldering ruins. All in all 349 buildings had been destroyed, and over one thousand people were left homeless. Some families lost everything they owned. Nothing was covered by insurance, because fire insurance did not yet exist in Boston. The fire victims had to rely on family and friends for food, clothing and shelter.

Eventually, Jeremiah and his family walked to a nearby village where his uncle lived. Here they stayed until they could return to Boston. The fire had taken their home and most of their belongings. Yet, they were lucky. They had a place to stay. Many families were forced to live in the fields and woods.

An investigation into the Great Fire of 1760 resulted in laws designed to prevent a repetition of the disaster. New buildings were to be made of brick or stone with slate or tile roofs. Streets were to be widened, and more fire fighters hired. Like Philadelphia, the city ordered more pumpers.

Some Puritan ministers interpreted the Great Fire as the "Lord's doing." They said that it was a punishment to the people of Boston for their "wicked ways." "Have not Bakers, Carpenters and other tradesmen been employed in servile work on the Sabbath Day?" one holy man reprimanded.

Following the fire, the city had to be rebuilt, but the money available for emergency relief and rebuilding was quickly exhausted. Boston needed help. A petition for financial assistance was sent to George III, but the king was indifferent to Boston's plea. Bostonians never forgot their monarch's neglect, and the Fire of 1760 helped light the fire of revolution in 1776.

It took many years for Boston to recover from the great fire. Jeremiah and his family were unable to return for five years. When they did return, they settled in another part of the city. But they would never forget the sight of Boston in flames.

A Fire on Pearl Street

Nine-year-old Lucy Tomkins and her younger brother had just given their father a good-night kiss when the bell rang out.

Mr. Tomkins ran to the window. A red glow in the eastern sky signaled a fire down by the waterfront.

"A fire! I must go at once!" he told his wife and children.

The enormous fire bell in City Park rolled back and forth calling the men of the New York Volunteers. From homes; from shops; from theaters and from restaurants, the Volunteers rushed toward Fireman's Hall. Once there, haulers pulled out the wheeled fire engine to drag it toward the disaster. Others grabbed buckets, hooks and ladders.

A small house tucked among warehouses was ablaze. Flames crackled along its timbers, and thick, black smoke poured from its windows. In the street children in night-gowns huddled together among the gathering onlookers. The Volunteer chief shouted orders through his fire-trumpet. Spouts of water, pumped by eight straining men, shot out from the engine hose onto the roof. Suddenly

RINGING THE FIRE BELL

there was an anguished cry. A woman came rushing out
of the building shrieking that her baby was still upstairs.
Immediately Mr. Tomkins hurried into the burning building. Within minutes he was back with the baby in his
arms. The crowd cheered.

Appropriately, the symbol of the New York Volunteers was the figure of a fireman holding a rescued child
in his arms.

The Volunteers were created in December of 1737
by the New York General Assembly. Thirty-five volunteers—"strong, able, sober and honest men"—were ap-
pointed. The man in charge of them was Jacob Turck,
a gunsmith. It was Turck who also designed the first fire
hat.

The Assembly instructed the Volunteers "upon notice of a fire to take the engines there and assist in its extinguishment and afterwards to wash the engines and keep them in good order." As the years went by, the Volunteers grew in number, and engine houses were situated about the city. The Volunteers became an important part of city life, enjoying the high respect of their fellow citizens. During the Revolution many of them served in the Continental Army and were with General Washington at Valley Forge.

In the mid-1800s the Volunteer system was succeeded by a paid fire department. For the 127 years of its existence, the New York Volunteers were more famous than any other American fire-fighting organization. A popular song of the time hailed their brave service:

> *His ladder placed against the wall,*
> *He quickly climbs despite the danger.*
> *Though in the scorching flames he fall,*
> *To fear he is no stranger.*

When Mr. Tomkins returned home, he was wet and tired. His clothing smelled of smoke. The Volunteers had battled the fire for over three hours. Although the house was destroyed, they had prevented the fire from spreading.

His family waited for his return.

"A friend stopped by to tell us that you saved a child," his wife said.

Mr. Tomkins shook his head.

"How wonderful!" Mrs. Tomkins replied.

Lucy and her brother beamed. They were proud of their father. He was a New York Volunteer.

Ruth and
the Firemen's Parade

Twelve-year-old Ruth Framer pulled her scarf tightly about her neck, protection against the cold and wind. Overhead, billows of gray promised a snowfall before evening. It was a raw February day in 1832. Yet, any discomfort was worth the wait. The Philadelphia Volunteers were to parade in honor of George Washington's Birthday.

Early firemen loved parades and pageantry. They needed little excuse to dress in their finest and march through the streets. Parades on the Fourth of July or on New Year's Day were commonplace. In 1825 the firemen marched to mark the opening of the Erie Canal. When General Lafayette visited New York City in 1824, the entire New York Fire Department passed in review. When Lafayette died five years later, another parade marked his passing. Parades could be miles long. One New York parade began about ten in the morning and did not finish until twilight the following day!

By noon, a crowd of over one hundred thousand people had gathered along Philadelphia's High Street. Excitement grew with the sound of distant bugles and drums. Ruth huddled closer to her mother and father. The crowd was overwhelming.

Before long, the first group of firemen marched by. They wore blue capes and white helmets. Behind them a group marched with their pumper. They were dressed in white uniforms with black leather belts and hats. Unit after unit, many from surrounding communities, marched by, each dressed in distinctive uniform. Many groups were accompanied by marching bands, whose members tootled on flutes and bugles.

The firemen had spent days polishing their engines and draping them with red, white and blue bunting. One engine carried a statue of George Washington, a fellow fireman, surrounded by garlands of evergreens.

The fire chiefs, marching in front of their units, were resplendent in fancy helmets. Helmets normally protected firemen from falling debris and splashing water, but special helmets were used in parades. These were decorated and gaily painted. The chief's helmet was always the most elaborate. One California chief owned a helmet of solid gold set with diamonds and rubies! A foreign visitor wrote home to Europe in 1831, "The American fireman on parade dresses more beautifully than any prince."

Ruth especially enjoyed the pumpers. Most were embellished with gilded scrollwork; hand carved orna-

mentation and paintings. No pumper was complete without a painting. Artists were hired to do the job. If the firemen could not agree on a theme for the painting, they left the choice to the artists. As a result the paintings portrayed a variety of subject matter. One portrayed Father Christmas smoking his pipe. Another showed a beautiful goddess crowning a heroic fireman with a wreath of roses. Still another pictured a landscape complete with wild animals and birds. Along with the paintings and scrollwork, the pumpers glistened with polished brass and glass-jeweled signal lamps. Many had mirrors set into side panels. It is easy to understand why the saying "All dressed up like a fire engine!" was once popular in America.

At one point in the parade, right where Ruth and her parents stood watching, the firemen gave a demonstration of their skill. A small wooden dollhouse was set on fire. Smoke poured from its little windows and doors.

Flames shot out from the shingled roof. A fire engine, pumped by eight men, turned its stream of water on the burning house to the delight of the spectators. Everyone cheered and applauded. Although Ruth enjoyed the spectacle, she thought it a waste of a lovely doll house!

Late in the afternoon the final unit marched by. The parade concluded with the Northern Liberty Company and their engine, nicknamed "The Red Crab." Just as they passed by, Ruth felt a touch of wet on her nose. It was snowing. If the snow continued, she could go sledding that night with her friends. It would make a perfect ending to an exciting day.

TWEED'S FIRE HAT

An Old Fireman Remembers

"I was a carpenter by profession and a Volunteer by choice. As a boy, I always wanted to be a fireman. Whenever a blaze broke out, I was there. I ran after the pumpers and joined in many a bucket brigade. Then I had my chance as a Volunteer. I joined the company in 1835. I was eighteen years old at the time. We had to follow rules, I remember them well:

> First, every volunteer is to help wash the pumper once every month as long as weather permits.
>
> Second, after each fire the pumper and all equipment is to be washed and stored.
>
> Third, any volunteer knowing of a fire and not reporting it within the hour is subject to a fine.
>
> Fourth, no excuse will be taken for neglect of duty except sickness or some family misfortune.
>
> Fifth, any volunteer neglecting his duty in any way for three times in succession will be taken off the list and replaced.

I cannot count the times I laid down my carpenter tools and rushed off to a fire. We were expected to be loyal and prompt. Our company motto was: When called, we serve.

I remember one winter night. I was in bed with a bad cold. The fire bell rang. I threw off my blankets and went to the fire. I forgot my cold and did my duty.

Another time I was called out on a bitter cold night. Everything was coated with snow and ice. We had to put runners on our pumper to pull it through the streets. At one point, the snow was so deep we had to tunnel through it.

I recall when the Empire Theater burned. For hours, the fire was beyond control. We had five pumpers at the scene. Citizens helped by drawing water from nearby wells and the town pump. But it was not enough. So, we pulled one pumper to the river and formed a line with the others. The first pumper pulled water from the river and pumped it to the second engine. The second pumped it to the third and so on, until it reached the theater.

Over the years I have been felled by smoke, drenched by water, seared by flames, frostbitten by cold, and struck by falling timbers. Why did I do it? Well, the love of excitement and knowing that your work is important."

"Pump Away, Boy!"

Miss Peterson had just called Ted to the blackboard when the church bell rang. The ringing of the bell on any day but Sunday meant one thing. "It's a fire!" Miss Peterson said. The children ran to the classroom window. In the distance they saw billows of smoke rising above Granny Martin's barn. She was Ted's grandmother.

"You may leave, Ted," Miss Peterson told him. "You may be needed."

"Thank you, ma'm," Ted answered. He left the schoolhouse and raced down the road past the scattered houses and barns of Springdale, Indiana. Springdale was a small farming community. It boasted one church, one school, one general store, and its own volunteer fire company.

When Ted reached his grandmother's farm, he found his parents and some neighbors hurriedly rescuing the livestock. His mother struggled with a stubborn cow, while his father carried a lamb to safety. Others chased sheep into an adjoining field or led frightened horses away. Poor Granny Martin stood by helpless.

"My chickens! Don't forget my chickens!" she cried out. But they needed no help. Two roosters followed by a flock of hens scurried across the barnyard to disappear under a shed.

Then, rolling down the road, "Big Washy" appeared, hauled by six men. Early pumpers were usually hand-drawn.

"Here comes Washy!" a man called out. "Get those buckets filled!" By this time, other neighbors had arrived, bringing buckets and pails with them.

Big Washy had come to Springdale all the way from Pennsylvania. The engine was built in 1795 by Patrick Lyon, a Philadelphia blacksmith. Lyon offered an interesting guarantee with his pumpers. He stated that if one of his engines ever failed, he would leave his grave to repair it free of charge. Such confidence was certainly justified. To this day there are Lyon engines still in working order.

The fireman stationed Big Washy near the barn. By now the smoke had turned to flame. Fed by buckets of water from Granny's well, Big Washy shot a cool stream onto the barn roof and washed down its sides. The men pulled and pushed the pump handles, trying to maintain a steady pulse. But it was too much for them. They needed help.

"Over here! We need some help!"

Ted was standing nearby.

"Come on, Boy! You're big and strong! Help us pump!" one man shouted. Ted rushed over and grabbed onto the wooden handle. With a sudden jolt he was joined into the straining rhythm of the firemen. Up and down. Up and down. Up and down.

"Keep her filled!" a fireman ordered as he directed Big Washy's nozzle. More water was dumped into her large copper-lined basin. This water was transformed by the pump into a forceful jet.

As Ted pumped, he saw his grandmother standing nearby.

"Pump away, boy!" she cheered. "You're saving the barn!"

With Granny's encouragement, Ted worked even harder. And his effort was worth it. The fire was soon under control.

BIG WASHY

The following week, the County newspaper reported:

A Springdale barn belonging to Mrs. Martin was discovered to be on fire about ten o'clock on Wednesday morning last. By the efforts of the local firemen, who brought their engine to the scene, the framework of the barn was saved. About one ton of hay and several bushels of corn were destroyed. The origin of the blaze is not known and damage is estimated at 600 dollars.

Back at school, Ted was a hero. Miss Peterson asked him to tell the class about his experience.

"I didn't do that much," Ted said shyly. "I just pumped away."

"Uncle Joe Ross"

A disastrous fire in Cincinnati brought about a drastic change in fire fighting. A city councilman, Joseph S. Ross, disturbed by the destruction caused by the fire, decided to give his support to a new idea. Two men, Abel Shawk and Alexander Latta, wanted to build a steam-powered pumper.

"I tell you, Mr. Ross," Latta explained, "our machine will replace muscle power with steam power."

"Think of it, sir," said Shawk. "A machine that will do the work of fifty firemen!"

Ross was convinced and arranged an appropriation of five thousand dollars to develop a steam-powered pumper.

When the Cincinnati newspapers reported the story, firemen ridiculed the idea. They said that it was a waste of tax money. "They want to replace us with a squirt machine!" one fireman charged.

But Shawk and Latta insisted that a steam machine would pump water faster and further than any crew of men.

The two men built their steam pumper. When it was finished, it was so heavy it required four horses to pull it.

Scientific American.

NEW-YORK, OCTOBER 25, 1851.   [NUMBER 6.

STEAM AND GAS FIRE ENGINE.

It weighed over twenty thousand pounds and had one wheel up front and two in the rear. Latta and Shawk named it the "Uncle Joe Ross" in honor of the councilman who supported their idea.

A public demonstration was scheduled for the new steamer. It was set for New Year's Day, 1853. Pulled by four big horses, the Uncle Joe Ross rumbled through the city streets belching smoke and sparks. When the steam pumper arrived at the city square, it was met by the volunteers of the Union Fire Company with their hand pumper. "We'll prove who's better," the firemen boasted. "We'll pump faster than any squirt machine!" Urged on by a large crowd, the two machines prepared for the contest. The steam machine huffed and puffed. The firemen started to pump. A stream of water jetted 200 feet. People cheered. "Hurray for the firemen!" a boy in the crowd shouted.

Next came the steam pumper's turn. It chugged. Water rushed through its hose and shot into the air. The pressure was so strong it took two men to hold the nozzle. The water hit a steady height of 225 feet. Some in the crowd booed and hissed. The firemen, seeing what the steam engine could do, worked harder. But the engine maintained its lead.

Then Latta and Shawk said, "Let's show them what else we can do." The engine was equipped with additional hoses. Soon six streams of water shot from the steamer. Here was a fire engine that did the work of six hand pumpers and needed only a few men to operate it.

The next day, the newspapers reported the story and hailed the Uncle Joe Ross as Cincinnati's champion. With fewer men needed to operate an engine, Cincinnati founded a city fire department with firemen hired as city employees. The volunteer firemen were angry. At one fire, the volunteers and the city firemen fought each other. One volunteer slashed the hose of the Uncle Joe Ross with his hatchet. Regardless, Latta and Shawk's steam engine was the fire fighter of the future. Soon other cities ordered steam engines and hired men to operate them. "We can run a steamer with a handful of men," boasted a Philadelphia councilman. "A driver; another to

stoke the engine, and a few to work the valves and hose. Who needs 20 or 30 men working a hand pump?"

By 1860 there were twenty-one steamers in the Philadelphia Fire Department, and Boston converted to steam engines. New York and Chicago also introduced steamers. Meanwhile engineers improved upon the design of Latta and Shawk. Lighter and simpler steam engines were produced.

The introduction of the steamer helped in the establishment of paid fire departments. With less manpower needed, cities and towns were able to support a paid department.

There were some volunteer companies who converted to steam, but many refused. Despite the obvious superiority of the steamer, many volunteers refused to use it. Perhaps they felt threatened by this newfangled machine. Pumpers needed men; steamers did not. As a result of this resistance, hand pumpers were manufactured in the United States until the early part of the twentieth century.

As one volunteer remarked sourly, "Keep your old 'Uncle Joe'! It's nothing but a big tea kettle!"

Peter Visits a Horse College

"Hurry, Peter, your uncle will be here soon!"

"All right mother," ten-year-old Peter Britton answered as he finished brushing his hair.

Peter's uncle was taking him to visit a horse college. At first, Peter had thought his uncle was joking.

"Honestly, Peter," his uncle had said. "There really is a horse college. It's where firehorses are trained."

Detroit claimed to be the only city that had a horse college. Fire fighters there had turned a former garbage dump into a training park. It was so lovely that it reminded some people of a Kentucky horse farm.

The use of heavy steam pumpers necessitated horses to pull them. Self-propulsion would arrive many years later with the gasoline engine.

In the beginning, fire fighters resented the horses. "A firehouse ain't no place for a stinkin' animal!" one fireman snorted. But the horses had to be kept there in readiness. Horse stalls became a part of the firehouse. The horses stood harnessed ready to go until the invention of the quick hitch. This device was a harness suspended from the ceiling by pulleys and weights. When the fire alarm sounded, it was dropped on the horses' backs. Before the quick hitch, harnessing took considerable time. With it, firefighters could leave the station within minutes.

Peter was amazed when he saw the college. It looked like a small village. There were several whitewashed barns and buildings. There was a fire station; there were training corrals, a horse hospital and a large, oblong racetrack.

"The horses here are very special animals," Peter's uncle explained. "Any horse can pull a buggy or a milk wagon, but a firehorse must be strong, clever, obedient and fearless."

Firehorses had to react quickly when the fire alarm sounded. They could not be timid or flinch when heavy gear dropped onto their backs. They had to be surefooted since they pulled heavy steamers along streets sometimes wet or slick with snow and ice. Though galloping at breakneck speed, they had to respond to the commands of the driver. Then, during the fire, they had to stand patiently despite the flames, the heat and the noise.

Fire fighters came to admire the firehorses. Soon, strong bonds of affection developed between the men and the animals. The name of each horse was painted above its stall, and the firemen often brought them treats of apples and sugar cubes. Some men even taught the horses to do tricks. A New York firehorse named Molly could catch a handkerchief tossed in the air and stuff it into the fireman's pocket.

Only the very best candidates for firehorses were brought to the college. After running at full speed, a veterinarian examined them for any weakness of muscle or heart. A horse that passed these tests was enrolled at the college and was taught all the skills it needed. Peter chuckled when a fireman told him that report cards were kept on each horse.

"What happens if one fails?" Peter asked.

"We have no failures here," the fireman answered. "Only successes!"

Peter watched as horses went through their training sessions. They were strong and efficient animals.

Peter especially enjoyed visiting the fire station at the college. It was a complete station and was used in the training of the horses. The ground floor housed the college steam pumper. In the rear, there were four horse stalls with hanging quick hitches. The second floor had a bunkroom and a recreation hall for the firemen. A

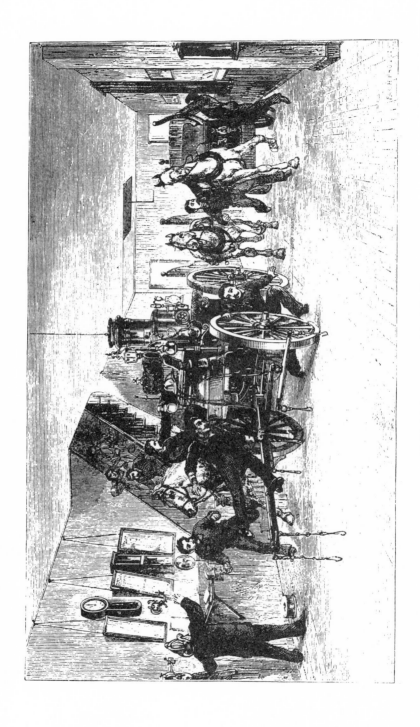

polished brass pole extended from the bunkroom, through a hole in the floor, to the ground level. When the alarm sounded, firemen could slide down the pole. These sliding poles saved precious time. One of the firemen allowed Peter to slide down the pole. It was great fun, and Peter decided to be a fireman when he grew up.

"You must come to our graduation next month," the fireman suggested. "Five of our horses are graduating."

At the end of training, the horses demonstrated their skills at a special ceremony. After graduation, some of the animals were assigned to other towns and cities to give on-the-job training to other horses. Firehorses lasted from four to ten years. It was a sad day when the firehouse veterinarian pronounced a horse unfit for duty. Some horses were retired to farms. Others were sold at public auction. The story is told of a milkman who bought an ex-firehorse at a sale. At the first sign of a fire, he would bolt off down the street leaving a trail of spilled milk and broken bottles.

To call someone "an old firehorse" was once highly complimentary. It meant that, despite age or infirmity, dedication to the job remained.

Leaving the horse college, Peter told his uncle that he wanted to be a fireman.

"Well, Peter," his uncle said, "like these horses, it takes long training and a lot of hard work."

"Save the Fat Lady"

Timmy was in New York City with his parents. July 13 was his birthday, and he had been promised a visit to Phineas T. Barnum's American Museum. The Museum was located at the busy intersection of Broadway and Ann Street. In 1865, it was New York's major attraction. People came from all over to see Barnum's sideshow marvels. Hugh posters plastered on the sides of the five-story theater described the wonders inside.

As he stood looking at the theater, Timmy could hardly believe his eyes. Were such things possible? There was a picture of Moby Dick, the Giant White Whale. Another poster showed General Tom Thumb, the world's smallest man, with his midget wife, Lavinia. Another featured the enormous figure of the fat lady.

"Look, Mother," Timmy pointed, "there's a picture of the giant woman!" Anna Swan, almost eight feet tall, was one of Barnum's leading attractions.

"We'll see it all once we go inside," his mother answered. "We can spend the whole day being mystified by Mr. Barnum's wonders."

"I especially want to see the animals," Timmy's

father added. Mr. Barnum's Museum was also a zoo. Its top floors housed hundreds of rare birds and animals.

The clock on the tower of City Hall struck 12:30. Timmy and his parents jostled along through the lunch-hour crowds toward the theater. Suddenly someone screamed. "Look! Barnum's is on fire!" Smoke and flames poured from the Museum's lower floor.

"Call for help!" someone shouted.

Timmy's parents pulled him to the safety of a doorway. "We better stay here until things are under control," his father ordered.

The Broadway crowds gathered around the building to watch. Museum visitors ran outside to safety, many screaming in panic. All was confusion.

Before long the New York Volunteers raced to the scene with steam fire engines. The firemen rushed into the building to rescue animals and performers. The fire had spread to the upper floors, and spectators cheered the courage of the fire fighters. Hundreds of birds were released from their cages. They fluttered through the dense smoke and out open windows. Other animals were less fortunate. Fire fighters mercifully killed animals that could not be rescued. Crocodiles, lions, snakes and a baby elephant had to be sacrificed. Moby Dick, the white whale, was killed. A tiger escaped from its cage and leaped from a second story window. The crowd screamed as the snarling animal plunged to the steet. A fireman quickly killed it with a whack of his axe. Except for a

MENAGERIE ON FIRE

seal, several monkeys and a few snakes, Barnum's entire animal collection was destroyed.

An eyewitness described the rescue of Barnum's human attractions:

> "A cry was heard, 'Save the fat lady!' The 400-pound creature was paralyzed with fright. Several firemen staggered under her weight as they carried her out of the building. Anna Swan, the giantess, had to be hauled out a window, and two midgets were brought out under a volunteer's arms."

The fire raged for several hours. By the time it was brought under control, the Museum and most of its contents were destroyed. That anything was left of the structure was credited to the powerful steamers.

Timmy and his parents watched as the tragedy unfolded. They witnessed the brave efforts of the New York Volunteers.

Unfortunately, it was the last fire for the Volunteers. Eighteen days after the Barnum fire, New York City instituted a paid fire department. The New York Volunteers passed into history.

By late afternoon on July 13, Barnum's was no more. Tumbled brick walls and smoldering embers were all that remained of P. T. Barnum's Great American Museum.

"It's a shame your birthday was ruined by the fire," Timmy's father said in sympathy.

But Timmy didn't mind. The excitement of the fire —the leaping tiger; the rescue of the Fat Lady; the bravery of the Volunteers and the shooting sprays of the steamers made it a birthday he would never forget.

The Tale of
Mrs. O'Leary's Cow

On Saturday evening, October 7, 1871, Mrs. Kate
O'Leary went to her barn. It was 8:30. Carrying a kerosene lamp, she entered the small frame building. Her
cows had settled in for the night and resented this in-
trusion. They balked as her lantern pierced the darkness.

Kate and Patrick O'Leary owned two cottages, one
behind the other, at 137 DeKoven Street in Chicago,
Illinois. The front cottage was rented to the Patrick
McLaughlin family. The O'Learys lived in the other.
Behind the O'Leary house was a small barn housing five
cows, a calf, a horse and a milkwagon. Kate O'Leary
ran a small business. She sold and delivered milk to the
neighborhood.

Her tenants, the McLaughlins, were having a party
and needed more milk for an oyster stew. Mrs. McLaughlin had asked Kate for a bucket of milk.

Kate O'Leary set the lamp on the floor and began to
milk one of her cows. The animal, annoyed by this extra
demand, began to kick at the bucket. Its hind foot
knocked over the lantern. Kerosene spilled onto hay and

ignited. Kate O'Leary screamed as she watched the fire spread. Her husband and the McLaughlins heard her and rushed to the barn. They tried to rescue the livestock but failed. The flames formed a blazing wall. Only the calf was pulled to safety. Other neighbors helped by forming a bucket brigade. But in the excitement, no one thought to turn in an alarm. More than a half-hour passed before an alarm was sounded. By 9:10 the fire had spread to other backyard barns and shacks.

Several fire companies responded. Horses were hitched, and pumpers were rushed to DeKoven Street.

At ten, a light breeze blew up and carried sparks and burning cinders with it. The steeple of a nearby Catholic church caught fire. Soon the church was in flames. Surrounding buildings and warehouses were next. By 11:30 the O'Leary fire had spread to Chicago's business district. Overworked fire fighters rushed from fire to fire while terrified and homeless citizens spilled into the streets. One eyewitness recalled that "buildings melted like snow." The heat generated by the fire reached more than three thousand degrees Fahrenheit. "Limestone was melting and running down buildings as if it were molasses." Chicago's mayor sent out a general alarm to other midwestern towns and cities—"Chicago is in flames! Send help!"

The city was in panic. Streets and roadways were jammed with a tangle of wagons loaded with furniture and bedding. People on foot struggled around them, screaming and crying. Others, crazed by fear or excite-

ment, ran wildly to and fro. Looters smashed store windows, making away with whatever they could carry. Everywhere, sparks and embers fell in a shower. One eyewitness recalled, "It was a day of terror and horror!"

Cathedrals, museums, factories, hotels and houses were engulfed in flames. Thousands of people rushed to the shores of Lake Michigan to escape the heat and smoke. Many, driven by the heat, went into the lake, and some were drowned.

At seven the next morning, the fire still raged. To make things worse, the city was running out of water. Wells were pumped dry. Fire fighters arrived from other communities but could do very little without water. Only a rainfall could quench the flames.

Nature came to the rescue on Monday evening, more than twenty-six hours after the fire began in O'Leary's barn. Rain poured down on the blazing city. By Tuesday morning the fire had finally died out. Seventeen thousand, four hundred fifty buildings were totally ruined, and nearly ninety thousand people had been left homeless. City officials and church groups organized emergency stations to care for the victims of the fire. Other groups cared for lost children and the injured. Few Chicago families escaped the scourge of the fire. Oddly enough, one of the few homes left standing was the O'Leary cottage. Chicago was furious.

Newspapers attacked the O'Learys, blaming them for the tragedy. Kate O'Leary changed her story. She claimed she had finished milking by four in the afternoon and gone to bed with a sore foot. Nevertheless, the tale of Mrs. O'Leary's cow persisted. "It's Kate O'Leary's fault!" people repeated.

"A stubborn cow and a careless woman have destroyed Chicago," one newspaper charged.

Despite the notoriety, Kate O'Leary and her family eventually faded into obscurity, but the story of her cow lives on.

Whether or not Mrs. O'Leary's cow really kicked over the lantern is uncertain. But the idea that the Great Chicago Fire broke out in the O'Leary barn is generally accepted. On the site of the barn, there is now a training academy for the Chicago Fire Department. And every year National Fire Prevention Week is proclaimed for the week in which October 8 falls—the anniversary of the Great Chicago Fire.

"Fire Ladies"

It was a warm spring night, and an almost full moon lighted the landscape.

Martha Hyer stood by her bedroom window. Although it was past midnight, she could not sleep. Perhaps it was spring fever or the thoughts of her upcoming eleventh birthday. The rooftops of Fairfield, Ohio, took on a silver hue in the moonlight. In the distance she could see the spire of St. Luke's Church and the bell tower of City Hall.

She also noticed a lighted window on Hill Street. It stood out in the darkness. When the light seemed to flicker, Martha realized that it was a blaze. A fire had broken out in someone's home. The people were probably asleep.

Putting on slippers and a robe, she ran downstairs and out the front door. Within minutes, she was pounding on Mr. Baxter's front door. He was a neighbor and volunteer fireman. An upstairs window raised, and Mr. Baxter leaned out.

"What's wrong?" he called out.

"Quick, Mr. Baxter! There's a fire over on Hill Street!" Martha answered.

"Run to the square and sound the alarm!" he ordered.

As fast as she could, Martha ran to the nearby square. She picked up the chained gong and pounded it against the fire bell. As it rang out, windows lighted and doors opened. Before too long the Fairfield Volunteers assembled at the firehouse and were off to Hill Street.

The next afternoon the *Fairfield Gazette* reported:

> The Wood residence on Hill Street caught fire during the early morning hours. Firemen quickly subdued a blaze caused by an overturned kerosene lamp. Young Martha Hyer sounded the alarm and saved the building from complete destruction. As a reward for her alert action, she has been named an honorary member of the Fairfield Volunteers.

Her parents were very proud of Martha. She had not stopped to awaken them but went straight to her duty.

"Now that you are an honorary Volunteer, I shall buy you a fire helmet for your birthday," her father promised.

As an honorary Volunteer, Martha was not unique. Women have played a role in fire fighting throughout its history. One of the earliest known female fire fighters was Mollie Williams. Born a black slave, Mollie worked with a New York Company. "She was a very distinguished volunteer," a comrade recalled. "Once during a blizzard in 1818, when only a few men got through,

Mollie was there. She struggled to pull the pumper through almost impassable snow."

Another female fire fighter was Marina Betts of Pittsburgh. As soon as a fire broke out, Marina was there. She became famous for her temper—dumping buckets of water over any man who refused to fight a fire. "They ought to be ashamed!" she said.

America's most famous female fire fighter was Lillie Hitchcock of San Francisco. She began her volunteer duty in that city when she was just a teenager. The community thought so highly of her that they gave her a diamond-studded fire-fighter's badge.

During both World War I and World War II, many women joined the ranks of fire fighters. With men at war, they assumed responsibility for fighting fires.

At a fire chief's convention in Chicago, one chief objected by saying, "No woman shall ever work in my department!" He was hooted and hissed into silence by the other chiefs.

In 1931, Nancy Holst became the first woman fire chief in America. She took charge of a Rhode Island company. And in Texas, there is an all-woman fire department led by a gray-haired grandmother. Recently, a Catholic nun on Long Island became a volunteer fire fighter. By a unanimous vote of the village trustees, Sister Sophia became a member of the Enterprise Hose Company.

Like young Martha Hyer, women have written their names in the history of fire fighting. As a veteran firefighter commented, "Not only do we have fire laddies, we have fire ladies!"

"Weber's Store Is on Fire"

The fire began through carelessness. Old Mr. Hanks had
been sitting by the pot-bellied stove in Weber's General
Store. He rested his lighted cigar on a cardboard box
while he gossiped with the other men. He forgot about
it, and no one else noticed. After the store closed, the box
caught fire. The flames ignited nearby baskets and
wooden crates.

It was almost seven in the evening when a passerby
saw the flames. He gave the alarm. All over Oakdale the
cry was heard, "Weber's store is on fire!"

The first to arrive was the Oakdale Volunteer Hook
and Ladder Company. A Hook and Ladder company
assists a hose or pumper company. In some communities
firefighters separated their responsibilities. Oakdale was
one of these.

In 1895, when Weber's burned, a typical hook and
ladder truck carried over three tons of equipment. There
were ladders, axes, hooks, rope and life nets. Three horses
running abreast hauled the truck to the scene of the fire.

The men placed ladders against the building. The
Weber family lived above the store and were trapped

there. One by one they climbed out a window and were brought to safety. Little Willie Weber, only two years old, was carried down the ladder by a "hookie." Even Lambie-Pie, the family cat, came down huddled in a fireman's arms.

While the rescue took place, other men broke through the store window. Dense smoke poured out. By now, Oakdale's pumper had arrived. The hose, coiled on a reel at the rear of the truck, was pulled out. Men dragged it to the broken windows. The pumper belched steam. Then the order was given, "Start the water!" A stream of water gushed into the store.

Three men were needed to direct the stream. Regular fire hose is two and a half inches in diameter. Oakdale's steam pumper pumped 300 gallons each minute. The weight and force of the water passing through the hose made it difficult to handle.

They watered the interior with the hose. The smoke was thick and black. Without the protection of modern oxygen masks, these fire fighters were true "smoke-eaters."

It took two hours to control the fire. By ten o'clock that evening, it was all over. The men gathered their equipment and reeled in the fire hose.

"We'll leave a few men here overnight," the chief told Mr. Weber. "They'll make sure the blaze doesn't start up again."

Mr. Weber thanked the chief. Through the efforts of his men, most of the building had been saved.

The Weber family moved in with friends until the

fire damage was repaired. Luckily, Mr. Weber carried fire insurance.

By 1895, fire insurance was available to everyone in all parts of the country. Over eight billion dollars worth of fire insurance was carried by American property owners. Benjamin Franklin's idea had grown into a big business.

Three months later, Weber's General Store reopened for business. On opening day, Mr. Weber sent each fireman a gift basket of fruit to say thank you for a job well done.

Fred the Firehouse Dog

No one knew much about Fred.

One fireman claimed that his mother had been a firehouse dog in a nearby town. Another said that Fred had been adopted by a former fire chief. Still another insisted that he was simply a stray who wandered into the town.

Nevertheless, Fred was the firehouse dog. He was a friend to all the firemen, and the company mascot. The spotted figure of the dog trotting alongside the horse-drawn steamer was a familiar sight in Annville.

Fred was a Dalmatian, a descendant of an ancient breed. The Dalmatian's beginnings date back to early times. A 1600 B.C. engraving shows a Dalmatian following a chariot. Roman and Greek manuscripts mention the spotted animal.

The Dalmatian is a "coach dog." Through the centuries the breed has learned to follow and guard horse-drawn vehicles. This instinct is bred into them. A coach dog's job is to protect the horses and to clear the path for the coach. Because of this tradition, American firemen selected the Dalmatian for their mascot. To this day, the sleek, handsome animal is also known as a "Firehouse Dog."

Whenever the fire bell rang in Annville, Fred responded as quickly as any fireman. He ran alongside the pumper making sure that the road was clear. Any person or animal in the way was ordered back by a sharp bark. And woe to an Annville dog who dared to snap or bark at the galloping horses! Although a gentle chap, Fred took his job seriously. When Bender's General Store caught fire, Fred exceeded his devotion to duty. He rescued Mr. Bender's kitten from the burning building. Carried out by the nape of her neck, she was dropped at Mr. Bender's feet. And, when the Goodson barn burned, Fred guided three horses to safety.

"Ain't he a great dog!" little Jeffrey Sharp remarked to his classmate.

"Yep! Fred is the best and the bravest dog in the whole world!" his friend answered.

All the children in Annville loved Fred. Sometimes he visited Annville's one-room school, curling up in a corner of the classroom. No one minded. Fred was a respected member of the community. One morning as he napped, the fire alarm sounded. Fred leaped to his feet and dashed out the open door toward the firehouse.

The pumper hitched, Fred raced alongside to the site of the fire. It was a minor matter. A pan of cooking oil had caught fire in Aunt Tillie Smith's kitchen. Fred returned to the school that afternoon.

While he was gone, the children made a paper fire

SITTING ROOM

helmet. On it the teacher
printed FRED THE FIREMAN.
They placed the hat on
Fred's head. His tail wagged
back and forth.

"Now he looks like a real fire fighter!" a child called
out. But Fred was a real fire fighter, with or without the
hat. Down through the years Dalmatians, like Fred, have
played an important role in the history of fire fighting.
They are well-known for their heroic performances.
Even today, when horses are no longer used, the Dalmatian is still an honored mascot of many a fire company.

The Night the Earth Rumbled

Twelve-year-old Peter Sanders recalled the early morning of April 18, 1906 in a letter to his aunt:

> I was awakened by the rocking of my bed. I jumped up and saw the floor and walls of my bedroom shake and shiver. Pictures fell and furniture skidded across the room. I heard glass smashing and a terrible rumbling. I called out for Mother and Dad. Then I heard the screams of women and children. I ran to my window. Outside, buildings swayed. Some crashed down with a roar. The street waved like an angry ocean. Dad rushed in and grabbed me. "Get out of here!" he ordered. The three of us went into the street and just in time. We watched as our home broke apart and fell down like a house of cards.

It was a little after five o'clock in the morning, when the earthquake hit San Francisco. The San Andreas fault, a crack in the earth's crust, was shifting under the city.

The movement caused buildings to tumble, streets to buckle, and water and gas mains to crack. It was a day of terror.

In Chinatown, superstitious residents threw money and valuables into the cracked earth. They thought that the wicked Dragon of the Earth was awakening from a long sleep. His waving tail was causing the earth to shake.

They hoped their offerings would quiet him. But the wicked dragon roared even louder. San Francisco was in deep trouble.

The earthquake was terrible enough. But fires broke out all over the city. Exploding gas mains and falling buildings caused hundreds of fires.

San Francisco's six hundred fire fighters did all they could. They not only fought the fires but rescued people trapped in the rubble of the earthquake. Yet in spite of all they could do, by the end of that day the many small fires had joined together into a three-mile-long blaze that swept across the city. For three days firemen battled the flames. Many of them dropped over from exhaustion. Companies from other California communities joined them, and the United States Army moved in to help.

The fire fighters struggled with a limited water supply and disaster all around them. They fought long and hard, but the fire raged on. The earthquake had lasted only minutes, but those few minutes caused many long hours of toil and suffering.

"Don't give up, boys!" their chief encouraged. "You've held out this long! Don't quit now!"

On Friday afternoon they finally won control. The spread of the fire was stopped. Then on Saturday, a rainfall drenched the city. The fire was over.

San Francisco was a sea of ashes. Over twenty-five thousand buildings were gone, and more than three hundred thousand San Franciscans were left homeless.

In his letter, young Peter Sanders continued:

When the rain came, we were so happy. It soaked the earth and killed the fire. We all felt sorry for the firemen. They worked so hard. Many of them were sick from the smoke and heat. The city was filled with homeless people, and we were among them. It was a time I will never forget.

The tragedy in San Francisco had some good results. In rebuilding the city, the public became more aware of fire prevention measures and demanded strict fire regula-

tions. The day the earth rumbled was a day many would never forget.

It has been said that the San Francisco earthquake and fire marked the end of an era in American fire fighting.

Shortly thereafter, the motor-driven fire engine made its appearance. With it came an age of mechanized fire fighting. Today's firemen use fast, effective equipment. A motor engine requires no heavy boiler. It is ready to start at an instant. The motor powers both the truck and the pumps.

In 1919, a small town newspaper commented on the town's purchase of a new engine. It is a proper conclusion to this story of firefighting.

Our city's new engine is a mechanical marvel. This gleaming red beauty will give us a safer community. But, we will miss the bellow of the steam pumper and the sound of horses galloping through the streets. Progress both gives and takes. It leaves us only memories.

Fire Fighting Museums

AMERICAN MUSEUM OF FIREFIGHTING
Hudson, New York

FRIENDSHIP VETERANS MUSEUM
Alexandria, Virginia

THE HALL OF FLAME
Kenosha, Wisconsin

TRENTON FIREMEN'S MUSEUM
Trenton, New Jersey

THE NEW JERSEY FIRE MUSEUM
South Orange, New Jersey

NEW YORK CITY FIRE MUSEUM
New York, New York

PHILADELPHIA FIRE MUSEUM
Philadelphia, Pennsylvania

OKLAHOMA STATE FIREMEN'S MUSEUM
Oklahoma City, Oklahoma

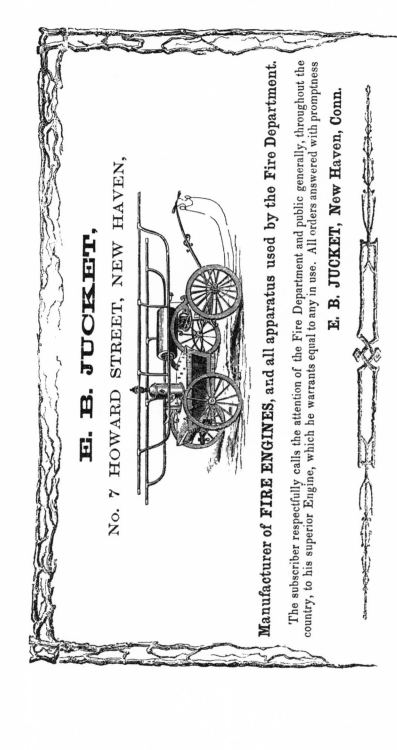

E. B. JUCKET,

No. 7 HOWARD STREET, NEW HAVEN,

Manufacturer of FIRE ENGINES, and all apparatus used by the Fire Department.

The subscriber respectfully calls the attention of the Fire Department and public generally, throughout the country, to his superior Engine, which he warrants equal to any in use. All orders answered with promptness

E. B. JUCKET, New Haven, Conn.

Bibliography

Americana Review. "The Volunteer Fire Department of Old New York." 1974

ASBURY, HERBERT. *Ye Olde Fire Laddies*. A. A. Knopf, New York. 1930

BLUMBERG, RHODA. *Fire Fighters*. Franklin Watts, New York. 1976

DeCOSTA, PHIL. *100 Years of America's Firefighting*. Bonanza Books, New York. 1964

DITZEL, PAUL. *Fire Engines-Firefighters*. Crown, New York. 1976

KENNEDY, JOHN C. *The Great Earthquake and Fire*. William Morrow, New York. 1963

SMITH, DENNIS. *History of Firefighting in America*. Dial Press, New York. 1940

SMITH, ELMER. *Firefighting at the Turn of the Century*. Applied Arts, Pennsylvania. 1971